The Naming of the Beasts

Ranald Macdonald

Chapman Publishing
1996

Published by
Chapman
4 Broughton Place
Edinburgh EH1 3RX
Scotland

A catalogue record for this volume is
available from the British Library.
ISBN 0-906772-78-8

Chapman New Writing Series
Editor Joy Hendry
ISSN 0953-5306

The publisher acknowledges the financial assistance
of the Scottish Arts Council.

Some of these poems have
appeared in the following magazines and anthologies:

*The Anthroposophical Review, Chapman, Cencrastus, Lines
Review,* and *With My Heart in My Mouth* (Steiner Press, 1994)

Cover design: Fred Crayk

Printed by
Econoprint
112 Salamander Street
Leith

Contents

In These Fields Far From Alone

In these fields
is silence
but for

the tapping of the aiglet
on the wall of my shoe.
And this hill too

is crowned with silence
broken only by
a telephone wire.

The voices in the wire
vibrate above
and beyond

the dykes
the sheep-dips
the crags

and be it from ever so far
the two ends of chat
are twined together

where otherwise only
blue sky talks
to clouds

and the sheer black sides
of night
echo to the gossiping stars.

The Naming of the Beasts

Adam named them
thoughtfully, knowing
he was right.

Today the beasts are named
and no-one would think to do it over again:
wisdom inseparable from wildfowl.

Even the unicorn has a name,
if not a posterity.
Though when it pauses to think things over
it calls itself the 'bereft',
'the earthless', 'the fable',
'beast without an earth beneath its feet'.

Adam had the power of naming.
Without him all the beasts would have gone
nameless, wandering naked, unherded,
through forest and glen till
gathered up by myth
to adorn the stories
of child gods.

Don't imagine there would be an earth
without Man. Though

through human malevolence
there might have been neither,
only a flood, dissolving itself in space.

–No twig, wrought by the dove
from the inchoate land. No land.
The dove eaten by the snake.
The ark unbuilt, because,
obedient to our heart,
the winds had come, the earth
quaked shut
on all human clay.

In the blank eye
of a unicorn's posterity
the light gleamed out.

In the Egyptian Section

A little black figurine with outstretched arms
and eyes set on a gaping distance – unscrutinizing
eyes, set in their own blue heaven, peering
down like Memnon over the flood-waters of High Nile.
One foot a pace ahead of the other; all
carved in ebony but all like a bone
in the ankle of a more comprehensive sun-walker,
striding high through wind and cloud
and moments of stacked sunlight.

Thus the Ka, the disembodied soul, goes
as will the most dissuasive of the dead
to the bird-light of Osiris.

Many Mansions

Zarathustra stared into the sun
for twenty years then spread the word.
Even at midnight and on cloudy days he stared,
with eyes shaped from light, and cloudless soul.
He spread the word, to Persians staring
blankly into earth, of Ormuzd and Angra mainyu,
Light and Dark.

Today for his pains Mazda is...
a light-bulb and a car. Ahriman
has no such trade name yet. His trade
lies in passing over into every name unseen.
Ahriman is in the brand name and the ad,
bristling with special offers.

I stared into the religion of the sun until
my eyes closed. I saw no Ormuzd
but in the darkness I did remember
lying in bed, seven years old and untouched
by seven-thousand-years-dead Zarathustra.
I was alone in an upstairs room.
I trembled. Angra mainyu came
into my dream, through the door
on a ladder with wheels.

The father, of my Presbyterian church, had left
His lower-case son in the bed (the bled-
white rock bed, the crust of the Earth
that my little soul stared blankly into: that bed).
It was as if the tune of unknowing was whistled
by a passing saint, footloose, down the corridors
of some freezing bloody Heaven that has no room
for a boy's home, or dog, or plastic suit of armour.

And Ahriman was in my church, He really was!
His skin of scaly stuff creeping from pew to pew.
Angra mainyu's pointed head appeared round every corner.
There he was in my school. He learnt
to read and write with me. Block-form
letters: a dead-garden alphabet of Apples and Balls,
far from the cuneiform of Zarathustra's Persians
who would have jumped like startled cats
at our writing and seen black magic there.

He is in our hardened arteries.
Angra mainyu is closing even
on the vessels of our blood.
All the mansions are His now
and in time He will come, spelling out
the wisdom of the Earth with letters
shaped from dark, and clouded soul,
to take possession.

Shake-Spear

If you say the word "shake-spear"
often enough, the man
who wrote plays
disappears behind the grass skirts
of a native
shaking a spear.
But if you say "renaissance" or
"rebirth" and fill your soul
with the flamboyant chorus of images
that the word conjures up, the man
materialises again and

however many times you say your name
you cannot make yourself disappear.

If I Were Valiant

If I were valiant
I would not stop
before the onslaught;
the slaughter
would not slow my blood
would not waste me on the field
to whiten in the gloom.

I would ride out
in the morning of a hundred years
if I were valiant –
I would shatter stone
and glint and know no bounds.
I would decapitate dragons
before noon of the first day.

A hundred years at least.

But a century
is another word;
it would stalk the stride of valiance.
A century lends its name
to burials and tumuli;
it is itself a grave
dismal in a stream of village midges
or forgotten on some hilltop –
      perhaps like dumplings in a stew
      mulled over
      in the minds
      of major-generals
      lately retired to Eventide Homes.
A century prohibits.
It would catch me in my drift.

A Spaceman God

His is the cathedral of the skies,
the stone of the random stars,
the battering of matter in empty
space.

Chambers of Commerce believe in Him,
Parliaments, Pentagons, Politburos
vouch for him, scientists
praise Him, without knowing
that from a pantheon of gods
they have picked the one
who has painted heaven black
in His descent.

He has tied His flag tight in the free-
flapping white heart of the gull.

The First Man in Space

is dead in a Russian grave.
But his brothers are still there,
poking the sunrise with their hands
and the sunset with their feet
simultaneously
as if tomorrow
would never come.

Bring me the night
alone in your brown
eyes unclench
my fists

and bring me
too gardens
of whatever
flower will release
its cataract life

into that space laid bare

of whatever flower
say rose
sighs into my ear
perhaps my mouth

bring what
you will

bring it
from the tensions
of such a well-tuned space

The Fallen Idol

So fast from round your shoulders
did I note the glad tidings
of that halo slip and fall away
through the dim beginnings, primeval
sorceries from which you first proceeded,
gathering the articles of lightened faith
with that brevity and decision of one
accustomed to standing in the starry world,

that now if I emit an unconstrained
slight lament or wail at this falling away,
do not, as I think you now may do,
misjudge or cast unsightly litigation
round my shoulders: they bear already
the dark rigour of allowing for
the fall of the illuminati, the bitter
castigation of letting slip away
the prosperous light. And this pain

strikes the hardest: not that one
who, stanchioned in the flight of gold,
fell to lead, but that I who saw
the faint elixir lift you to a high
electric pitch must now relinquish
all I thought I loved. Each night now

I make a tryst with the solitary dark
that, though all saints may not fall,
at least my stoic aspirations will not
crumble to the clouded dust with those that do.

Like One in the Wilderness, in Solitude

I am the wolf's breath, of vapours
the most alone, the most animal,
I am upon your shore the dusk,
the face upon your face of sand,
I am at your marble the dream,
the vision of green at your limbs,
I am at your mouth the glass,
the unclouded face you will catch.

More lucid than your face of passage,
most frozen glass, I am
the last, the most alone bestiality,
the stainless breath.

17

Sagittary

Said the young man to the centaur,
– From where do you come
  On what do you live?
Said the centaur to the young man
– I have always been coming,
  I live on honey and blood.
Said the young man to the centaur,
– Why do your hooves raise the dust?
  Why do your eyes not look down?
Said the centaur to the young man,
– How should I stop raising dust?
  My hind legs beat up the storm.
  How should my eyes look down
  when my path is ahead?
Said the young man to the centaur,
– Will you teach me the secret of honey and blood?
  Will you show me the way ahead?
Said the centaur to the young man,
– I will teach you the secret,
  I will show you the way.
Said the young man to the centaur,
– What must I do to learn?
Said the centaur to the young man,
-- To learn you must follow me now.
Said the young man to the centaur,
– Your hooves beat up the dust,
  your hind legs raise the storm,
  how should I follow you now?
Said the centaur to the young man,
– Follow me now.
Said the young man to the centaur,
– I have no wisdom, I have no path, all is dust.
  How should I follow you now?
Said the young man to the centaur,
– How should I follow you now?

Shades

Your soul, mounting
irregular exhibitions
in your eyes,

gave notice
of an exquisite strain
impending. (Violins

at pains to stay on top
with just that little bit more
vibrato

sometimes damage the air
and break down
screeching.)

The exhibition closed,
you went away,
I drew back

my outstretched hand
and turned to watch the sun
make playthings of the trees.

Weeks later you came back,
eccentric, trembling,
and wearing shades.

No longer did I see
exotic landscapes, like smoke
twist back in your soul;

no longer did the sun,
like a lathe, turn
innumerable smiles

on the row of portraits
all the way down
behind your stolen eyes.

A Death in December

In the rosebed,
livid that such a succulent
portion of my dream
should go to the palsied wasteland,
I clipped the only rose left in December,
almost praying for it
to rise up against my hand
or foment revolution
in the name of good to save its skin
and pierce mine with a thorn.

But the rubber glove came down
like a cold compress on the sickly thorn
and nowhere could the briar
twist back recalcitrant
from the snip of the secateurs.

And all the time I knew
that you
in your deserts and gruff funereal canyons
would decimate the lilt and grace
of this flower's voice; that you
would make rough the skein of light
and drown in sand the ancient figure of love.

I had no heart for this
and would not tip a rose into your grave.

Instead I set the rose afloat
in a shallow stoneware bowl
and framed a hope against the sun
that before all flesh was done
some secret essence would sail
into the balm of Osiris
and away from the stiff ligament of death.

Whereas you – please go
with no reluctant token.
I simply wish you well
and won't substantiate your going
with more than this.
You are now out of substance.

And I wish
for the quick extirpation of all your sorrows.

Ghost

the ghost
of my right hand
gropes for and tickles
the palm
of a fox-glove
which is merely
a spectre as well
in the land where
words introduce themselves
informally
and ghosts shake hearts

An Exercise of Will

1

A three-tier stove topped by wrestling bears:
each day I move the bears
from the stove to the desk
at ten past seven in the morning.

It strengthens the will
and God grant us many
strengthened wills by the end of the day

or the bears will chew our spines.

2

When I was wee
bears chewed my spine nightly
and I drowned in the pillow.
Once it was wolves
who came through the door on a ladder with wheels
and once I saw many monsters in the church –
how they gathered their scaly wings around my father
who was dead.
I asked for sixpence to get a bus home.

Now that I am home
I must wonder what to think
when my father says, "I have found the Lord".
It is all a dream but is he really in the church?
Am I really skating on thin ice in the snow?

3

What do monsters think?
I will ask them tonight in my sleep.
Let them only speak.
I shall harness their claws and wings.
They shall gnarl my spine and twist the muscles in my back
but let them speak.

Theirs is the wisdom of caves and engines
sacred to my other heart
and I will give them my ears
though they will surely eat them.
Do monsters think as much as angels sing?

Escape by Night

Outside the train   darkness
This compartment is my compartment
Nothing to change it   nothing
It carries my home   snail's
shell unspiralled between stations

Forests of dark crowd upon the train
Trench-coated trees with night
occurring in their cases   creased
in their lapels   A gendarmerie
Take them on board?   Speed by
Speed   by

In the Therapeutic Community

Sitting on the patio with Peter, whose obesity
seems to grow by the minute, splitting
his trousers over and over again
(prodigious feats of eating are achieved
by raging infants in the skins of men),
the patio also splits:
flakes of cast-iron rust and Victorian stone
mingle on the ground,
petals of a real-world cherry-blossom.

We wait together for the day to grow older.
(Nights there were as well and stars.
Our youth melted like wax around a wick
and, losing our place in time, we found
our time and place in the spinning stars.
Jupiter, Saturn and Mars
dizzying the Virgin,
confabulating the affairs of men.)

But it is lunchtime and Paul comes out
breaking up Battenburg cake for the birds.
I tell him the marzipan will gum up their beaks.

Peter is writing a love-letter for Joe.
(Joe can't write and is in love with Lynn,
who can't read.) But feeling restless Peter
looks up and says,
"Every building but ours has had a face-lift".
It's true. The neighbour's grime is gone,
blasted off, and now like time or sin
it drifts in little wells and eddies
along our unredeemed sills.

Paul has gone upstairs and trying to think
of something therapeutic to do throws
polo-mints down from an upstairs window.
(There's little enough healing
in this hebephrenic household.)

The sky, which never gets the heebie-jeebies,
throws up a great therapy over this old
tobacco-baron's lodge and over the new
buildings too, the University.

Cultureless, the uni. can't hear that far,
can't feel the healing.
Instead, a forcible mallet rises
in its architecture
to pound the innocent blue.
(Innkeeper's rough rebuttal to Mary.)

Only the sky remains intact, innocent,
culturing no history in its tubes.
Far better now to send out gulls, clouds, snow,
anonymous mist, than indulge in history.
Personless, caseless, no I, no you
in the grammar of clouds.
No genitive, no possessive, open.

Not like our hearts, in which 'I' and 'you'
are always turning into cases
of possession and plunder.
(Are closed books too, unless the sky
or other restoring kindnesses
impinge upon their cover.)

So we might as well just sit here
while the Victorian in our skins
crumbles away; while the university
in our brains withers the cerebral blooms.
Head, the former image of the cosmos, now impacted.
Too pawky to be human,
too angered and febrile to be animal.
Too bastardised to be divine.

Glasgow crumbles, unable to bring forth designs
to match its delights. Its folk
fall into a delinquent twilight,
gainlessly unemployed.

And with an almost Hebraic facility
for making the solution synonymous
with the riddle we wait here for ourselves
to emerge from the conundrum.
Derelict, unhealed, hurting
each other for fear that Christ
or Whoever shall Save
may not light up in us but rather
that some igneous fiend is our inheritance.

God knows the answer but He too
is schizophrenic and won't give it straight,
throwing Polo-Mints from an upstairs window.
But then, "Man is also the religion of the gods",
and we would throw them straight
back up again but for gravity
which is science
not religion.

observed that life had lost its tumultuous forests, its storm,
its floating horizons
found it to possess no more inky nights, no distant visions
Shelley, on remembering the story of the witch whose
nipples were eyes,
shrieked and ran out of the room holding a candle
so flinging back ghosts into the periphery of this hardened shell,

I expunge them
and allow once more untold electric storms, vast
purgatories and palaces of spirits to approach,
ghostlike and reeling from without

The Broken Pane

I broke a window with a golf ball
I'd thrown all the way from the bottom of the garden.
Dripping with guilt I went up to it.

The edges of the glass
were green
like frozen lime-juice.

A teacher had said
glass was made from sand.
I didn't see how, it was more as if

leaves and grass were locked in the panes.
A long time later I wrote a poem about seeing
the green eyes of God

in a rock-pool. The ragged edges were draped
with moss, many different shades of moss:
bottle-green, diluted lime-juice green, spring-bud

green, and pink, clinging like soapless sponge
to the glazed surface of the rock (granite,
itself still pink

from a time before the Flood, before
the pulse of stone had hardened). Yes,
God's eyes are green and I

like a spy observed Him
climbing out of a rock-pool.
The water rang like crystal.

"But how did you know you were naked?"
asked God in a fit of temper, His green eyes
flashing. Adam squirmed. Forgetting

the fact of my own nakedness (knowledge
that makes me stupid) I gazed at God's'
as it was revealed

in His eyes. The rock-pool shimmered;
down the edges of my soul ran a streak of green
like marble embossed in quartz.

I looked out on a pristine world
and loved it. God
may see His world from rock-pools;

through a human soul, with that sense of belonging
only a creator can identify,
He may love it.

Nothing comes
between us

but through an open door

between us
nothing comes

Snake of the Willow and Its Shadow

Snake of the willow and its shadow,
The bluebird is acquainted with your throat
And desists.

Snake of the willow and its shadow,
Does your tongue tune the fronds
Which quiver in the space of filmlike blue?
Does any bird of unheeding fly
Within those strands, that hair of death?
I wonder if there is any love fit enough
For your initiation, Snake Shaman.

May be only the sad and the worn, whose lips
Have tasted death, and blackened, will come
To your circle. Only the flowers
Of a rainlike sorrow know your oracle,
And they have withered.

Not sad, not worn, not friends of the little dead,
The bluebird and I we fly to you still
For your weeping heavens, for your high knowing
In the eye of the sun. But, already falling,
We have thought too much, and our thoughts
Seem like your curtained mansions,
Low snake, low willow, low shadow.

For a Pulmonary Religion

It must be sketched upon water,
inscribed upon flame,
entered in respiration.
It must go down into your heart
by that lake to fashion
the berthing-place of stars.

It must implant storm
at the floor of all things,
that when the seed comes through
its own full mouth
it will flower thunderclouds
and scatter ions across the stubble-plains.

And at that still unopened lake
there is a haft of steel
you must grip: take it,
the unstained blade
must make swaths of the night
until stars again stravaig
the great oceans of sky.
Same stars
berthed at your heart
ranged across the sky.

The Equal Nights

The changing of the clocks
forward
through vernal
equinox

> (spring
> soul opening there
> like sound of ah
> to the round
> of swirling stars)

squares
our faces to the
summer
solstice and

the ebullient
sun
leaps up over
the tenements

> (which former
> captains
> of shadow cast
> down into our one
> receptacle room
> pails of winter).

In the Botanic Gardens, Glasgow, Persephone

penned memos to Demeter
on the back of dog-rose petals
and floated them down the river,
to flirt between ripples. It was spring
and her writing was like
a tickling on the back of the knee.

Hades, on the bed of the Kelvin, saw
the petals float by and gave out
a cry meaning 'life' and meaning
'lust', like a raven's caw,
a noise cowled from the black
ornamental railings and funebral pathways.

"Bring me to that life again!" he cried,
stealing the last kiss from the sunset,
hurling the light from the pale dog-rose
down into his heart.

A little later Demeter came out again
amongst the traffic of the Great
Western Road and heard her daughter's
myth, tussling in the dank
internal combustion for a place
in the sun.

And further down the road a small boy
walked right through her,
the shadow under his chin darkening,
as if it had never reflected buttercups.

Bath

The wind took a bath
in the trees thinking
not to be seen but
I was there and heard
how the tub creaked
like a legion of Romans
hiking the treadways
of England and splashing
its soul with cruel branches.

Balin and Balan

An electric storm
rumbled
down this way

just as I had my finger on the light-switch.

I stood aghast
while its mass
came baleful
through the window.

Balin and Balan
hid in the green-dark
forest when storms like this
were conjured against them

and I too would jump beneath the bed

but for my eyes
strictly given
to reflect the lightning strike

and my pale receiving
form
hewn from the godhead
at one dolorous stroke
to be filled with the smoke and rumble.

The Great Conjunction

Jupiter and Saturn – Proper Names.
And – a conjunction that brings them together
thrice: a great conjoining in the womb of the Virgin.

> Little fathers, what will become of us now?
> On the face of the earth we tremble
> before the sign in the face of the heavens.

> We are not equal to that face;
> we cannot dispel with our youth
> the many wrinkles falling from the brows of the gods;

> we cannot deflect the patrimony that falls
> with a bad grace or feed
> on the gift that will not sustain.

> Little fathers, is darkness the light we shall follow now?
> We tremble: Darkness and Light
> wrestle in the womb for which shall be first born.

I quietly slip away from the stars' diverse action
to walk in earthly places, familiar bazaars.
Many items change hands. I change hands
more times than I like to remember.
At each new lodge I check
for the action of the stars against the faces of men.
A shadow or dark miasma checks
against their faces for a questionable moment.
And suddenly I go through, am turned out
into a playground.

For this I had slipped away.
For the playground.

More equally, for Zeus and Hermes
not to have walked among men
was for the stars to have gone cold in their spheres.

> If I were to do a painting of those faces of men and
> women
> I would call it 'Children with Plums'.
> Not 'Playground'.
> I would want people to look on it and think
> 'Playground'
> for themselves.

Perhaps among those faces you would see
the broad features of Zeus,
the quick expression of Hermes.
No idle bystanders they but active innocents.

From the playground you can see naked
the Great Conjunction of Jupiter and Saturn.
Or you can play.

Blue   Winter Blue

The train pulled away
with the window half down
and the monastery compartment
echoing to its stone
with tears   A small hand

waved   Stone-faced solitude
carried me back back
back   The train waxed
in the fullness of departure

I looked on receding
into an inner distance growing
smaller and smaller until
reconstituted   a wisp
of smoke in a stationless
landscape
Blue   Winter blue

Letter to an Egocentric Friend

Friend,

Only the oldest and surest belief holds
that the most wise source, the most eternal flame,
pertains to the centre: the cyclotron sun;
the god Amon-Ra who sits there; the tiny nucleus,
plotting whole organisms from its cell; the spirit; the heart;
truth.

My very dear friend, we always neglect the edges.
Oh yes, we've been told all good things come
from the heart, as if the edges were rough, spoiled,
unhappy – blighted with fallen angels and irrepressibly
sinful humans.

But it's an old belief, essentially: centrally old.
Stop believing it... like Columbus you'll fall off the world.
Open it up and... well, perhaps it's like an ageless priest,
wound up through time in the mechanism of his god:
perpetually he descends the spiral staircase to matins;
constantly the crack of dawn wakes the flagstones
with a chill of light; forever a dying god stretches
and brightens in his window. Always.

Let's not stop at this, but consider:
central to you is your ego. Forgive me for saying
you're famous – famous for basking there, like
a sumptuous lion. And though you seem to think
the continued burning of the sun depends on the way
you shake out your mane, that's not important.
As someone himself off-centre let me tell you
your periphery's magic.

Earth, air, fire, water, they all flicker there
with the elemental delight only nature can sustain
in her favourites. Rain, lightning, wind, the moist earth,
all send their agents to your vicinity.
And from the outside in, elemental beings
have joked you into love.

Elementals? Sylphs, undines, salamanders...
how long is it since everyone saw them?
So many centuries castles have crumbled since.
Gnomes dressed like medieval peasants, isn't that

how we see them? That's how long it's been.
But we don't see them, we imagine them away.
And they, poor creatures, can't withstand
the indifferent heat at our core.

But what they have done is to weave a laughter-
filled sorcery about you and to ensure it has
no core. And that, my friend, is what saves you
from yourself.

Mine is the eccentric line and I cite you
as my most unlikely champion.
The magic around you has no origin –
it always played there,
free of beginnings.
Let origins, centres, hearts fall away.
Think of Saturn. Cold and distant, rare and fine,
a thought brightened only by rings. Rings
outstretching this poor imagination.
A picture now faint with distance, a timeless beauty
flung out to the farthest reaches.

Love, your eccentric friend.

Father

The trees are cold the night is dark
When I meet father in the park
He asks me why I gawk with dread
I say perhaps because he's dead

Now he's returned from foreign lands
To split the night with frozen hands
I ask him why he's been away
He tells me that he cannot say

But that he'll lead me from this place
That where we'll be I'll have no face
And I must follow where he treads
To mix with those who have no heads

The Greatest Aim

the greatest aim
is sleep
so deep

that the living
beasts
rubbing their flanks

against
slumber
will only

make it
shake off
the drops

of dream
in some still
deeper pool

The Cat's Eyes, the Threshold

Snow began to fall.
Walked on, into the gloom,
> eyes
> opening
> like darkling stars
> one
> by
> one
black sequins emerging all
down the roadway, they were cat's eyes.

At the lapse of each interval would be
a cat. Cats
at intervals: cat   cat   cat one
and all posited where some dread thing lapsed
into the familiar
curling form.

*

A cat makes a station
between who-knows-what regions
just by sitting:
where the cat sits the mystery
of the world to which we are strange
bursts through, is impressed
upon our domiciled vision like
a purple fruit.

Now comes the stranger to the threshold.

There are
layers of worlds, layers and layers, where do you begin,
behind ours, another
to which we are strange,
we strange
to it, it strange
to us,
the cat's eyes, the threshold.

Worse: this world
which rising from the laminations seems ours
may not be ours at all or what it seems but only
where strangeness walks.
A seeming world become beneath our eyes

the inhabitation
of darkly crawling species. Black what
scuttles though spaces, verbs?
We do not see
our world is mezozoic, teeming
with a purpling strangeness.
And where cats walk
there is a dealing
between household and alien.

*

Without even shifting their locus
the cats were stealing feathers.
What stealth! Unbelievable!
But we are so slow and unbelieving.
The eye is deceived. Like a grape it is not active.
Stays with the pear and apple
while all the fun goes on and stealth
with cats, who are constantly stealing.
Hades by stealth gets Persephone.
Who is innocent? – Who is ripped
from the fauna to be taken
in god-knows-what voluptuous fire?
May be too much sun in her ripening breast.

Feathers?
There was a crow, it was
the creature on the inside of the bulbous world.
And the shiftless cats stole its feathers.

The crow veered into a canyon,
the canyon closed its mouth.
At the mouth closing
the sky began to rise.

the sea was so calm
I could
        sit in the shadow of its foam
        and still discern
        the whisper of a seal,
almost certainly
a human soul
        enchanted,
        in death perhaps though
if you sit
in the shadow of its element
its words may sound
before it returns
        to its green death-waters.

dead, it was of
the 'dead' – say it
softly
for spitting the doleful sound belies
        the ringing life
of this word: the 'dead' lives
        in the vibrancy
        of some deep word-lake;
the dead live

Standing in the Moondust

Standing in the moondust
of a valley in the Sea of Tranquillity
quite alone quite desolate I
considered the crescent earth

The shadow of my left hand
eclipsed Naples
of my right foot
occulted the eastern shores
of the Mediterranean

But I would prefer
to restore the gold
to the blackened haloes of saints
in the paintings of Giotto
than to mastermind
a thousand-and-one total eclipses

Green Light – The Sunken Garden

1

Long ages. Sleep, wake again, sleep.
Green light – the sunken garden
is radiant, the work of angels.
Darkness falls like a bird without form
through a clenched fist.
And blackened, the garden withdraws
into the last vestigial light
on the face of the green pond.
Pralaya, a great sleep.

Light, passing over, is to this soul,
the Angel of the Passover,
marking our doors with the holy residue of breath.
There is a fire in our lungs.

Who am I, who sleeps, who dies,
who opens to the wind, a full-rigged ship,
who closes to the sky, this clenched fist unmourned?

2

The angel of life within me shapes a separate face.
Green light fares across, I wake, celibate,
and slake myself with greed through its green throat:
I am the old pond,
great ages subsist in my crumbling stone surround.

And you – oh, you are in the golden leaf
that floats all that way down unseen sliproads
to fall out here, contiguous palace of the stranger,
garden of secret death.

So is the light across my face
made all a gift to that leaf.
So you, your life, your focused light
will play upon my surface.

3

We suffer change, have now the life of children.
A green vase, our work, slips from our hands
and we sleep, suddenly brightened.

Immediate as the Farmroad

and
immediate as the farmroad woke me walking down
it came
with starpoint sharpness
swooped through the mist to the night sky
that
the shock precipitate of mind
plopped into matter
was
into the mist foot by foot descending
into the next word through darkness dropping
myself

Riddle

What comes into being
every time you sit down?
Your lap.

And now, with the lap composed
by a riddle,
I, like our cat
who knows which lap is most faithful,
will rest my head there.

They say, It is in the lap of the gods,
that human hopes are committed to
the lap of the gods
and gain their commission there:
                aspirations waver
                then are blessed,
                genius trembles
                then is touched with light or dark,
                destruction
is torn into the earth from there.

But if my head is cold and fruitless
and I cannot pluck the grapes I want
or wear the wreath,
(words fail me
and the poet's economy is broken)
then the gods seem frigid,
Memnon at High Nile,
forbidding and remote.

Now here begins a personalised
mystery for
                this lap in which
                a smooth hand
                filled my writing-
                head has gone to stone

                and I climb down
                to make a shadowy passage
                between the roasting
                elms and beef

                of this day
                Sunday, now
                and forever

                sad with echoing children
                beyond the pond and the fishing boys.

a dead red leaf
cuffed by the wind
and stalked by a ginger cat
I was turned by the wind
till my veins showed through
dried in the bones
of a dead red leaf
I was turned by the wind to poetry

for one touch of your hand
I would be torn
by the claws of a ginger cat
I would melt my substance with the earth
for one kiss of your lips
I would leave death to the earth
and write no more

Michael and the Dragon

Six hundred and twenty-five lines
in a television picture.
Sixteen frames a second in a film.

No frames or lines at all in this room
just a table/chair/bookshelf/picture on the wall
of St. Michael slaying the dragon.

And in the chair myself
making a poem of it all.
But it's a poem already,
etched in the lines of the commonplace.
St. Michael somewhere in the act
of composition, the dragon disputing it,
that the room should stay inarticulate.

A simple room brings you
to yourself and returns proportion
to itself.

"Isn't it real, just like TV?"
That is the beginning of the end.
Having never been on television
the contents of this room might wonder
just how real they really are.

The room shivers, suddenly prosaic.
St. Michael pales, the dragon
withdraws to the picture
but stays in the room.

this darkness belongs
not to the absence of snow
but to the magical
dilution of icicle squash
in a land beyond
all bootstraps

No Taking You from This Homeland

These few sparing pangs
brought fresh heart,
carried you inland.

Though not on my shore
you are constant, so
on my shore.

No more to say I went
    to fetch my supper.
    Now when I got there I found

    the cabbage inedibly dead.
    Dead but from its shoulders
    sprouting a new cabbage, nape to crown.

This food I ate,
this love we take
will bear us over these dead fields.

doubtless the balance of all things
sweet hangs on the green
of your steel
grey eyes

as I walked past
the mortuary
I saw a note
pinned to the door
it said
teacher
give to the poor
and the dead
it said
do not give
credence
to the flimsy
hungry day
but
I was a week
late for my lecture
and could not
stop
for the whims
of the stiff

In the Taxidermy Workshops

The tiger in the fridge, as yet
unstuffed, roars no more, is
no longer Royal Bengal, has seen
vistas of the interior
invert, passing through the captor's
eye like wholly unreal camels.

Even a unicorn might be here:
a stuffed myth.

And here, this coelacanth –
surely the last –
has a dream caught in its eye.
Dreaming in primeval vision
its own extinction it fell
too far asleep and came
out ready-stuffed
in the museum-case:

tidings
of a deep, less deep.

Purgatory

A landlord of sorrowful eyes
came to my door

Tears slithered down the cups of coins
A penance of holy water

Sweltering in the beasts of purgatory
I would think often

of those cool dilutions
'Paid in like kind'

Reincarnation

High trees sway, corn grows tall,
determined to add to the country's store
of sweetness, flies buzz dementedly:
reincarnations of the thoughts of men.

The hot sun strokes heads
unremittingly, ideas dip and soar,
embodying themselves in the flight of turkey-buzzards,
in the feet of little children splashing in paddling-pools.

I have been here before, I say to my dreams,
to my night-thoughts, picturing
wakeless deaths and squalling rebirths,
I have been here before. And

slap! A thought that rested on my leg
to irritate escapes again: one more
bright invention zips and tears above the clover,
insinuating itself into the presence of flesh.

Unicorn

If I were a beast of the field
I would be a beast
of the airy frieze:

a unicorn
nuzzling the world
for its existence,

nowhere able
to be more
than imaginary,

goading a rarefied mate
with its horn
that by some elemental

act of reproduction
it might
drop

from the mythical ether
into the coarse
deliberations of earth.

we bring
new monocles for one-eyed priests
we bring
buttons for old coats
typewriters for literate spiders
alarm-clocks for angry boys
old stings to sound out dock-leaves
light-bulbs for suggestive tomes
a taper for the candle
   somewhere not found in the infernal machine

and shaking you by the left hand
we urge lightning where thunder is only
we give you no lights bound with sense

full-fast from a blaze of firs in our mind
we bring unaccommodating words
over the top of the trenches

for the lakes are burning
and the couch-grass sizzles
and hormones are hell-hot
fired with the vision of doors left open
   in musty mansions

and we are not stapled to the page

Inventory

1 stationary-cabinet
2 escritoire (without key)
3 blotting-paper
4 clock

5 fresh raindrops on the window-pane and
6 an orange street-lamp dilating them
7 my eyes on the vacant window
8 dark night (without key)
9 Isobel,

sitting on the heater, breathes
as if she were asleep. She isn't
but her comatose lungs respire
like a sleeping forest – a forest
of Middle Earth, dim homeground
of the ogress Baba Yaga
or the princess who danced by night.

Isobel: fourteen years in an asylum,
a chocolate house she ate her way out of.

The air bends inwards. Night two
of the thousand-and-one nights
was just as dark. I think

poetry is
sight to the blind,
a shoulder to grip,
teeth to shred
this inventory world of things.

Isobel drops her comb:
a forest leaps up
to stall the lunging ogress.

Biographical Note

Ranald Macdonald was born in Edinburgh in 1955. He studied English at Aberdeen University, followed by Speech and Drama in London. He has worked in a therapeutic community in Glasgow and, after a training in the work of Rudolf Steiner, taught for a number of years in the Aberdeen Waldorf School. His poems have been widely published and in 1990 he received a Writer's Bursary from the Scottish Arts Council. A pamphlet, *The Only Ankles for Midges to Bite,* was published by the Lapwing Press in Belfast in 1994, followed by a book for children, *Tales from a Tall Islander* (The Children's Press, Dublin). Ranald Macdonald is currently living near Belfast, working as a teacher in the Holywood Steiner School.